How To Make Money On Instagram

HTeBooks

Disclaimer

This book is designed to provide condensed information. It is not intended to reprint all the information that is otherwise available, but instead to complement, amplify and supplement other texts. You are urged to read all the available material, learn as much as possible and tailor the information to your individual needs.

Every effort has been made to make this book as complete and as accurate as possible. However, there may be mistakes, both typographical and in content. Therefore, this text should be used only as a general guide and not as the ultimate source of information. The purpose of this book is to educate.

The author or the publisher shall have neither liability nor responsibility to any person or entity regarding any loss or damage caused, or alleged to have been caused, directly or indirectly, by the information contained in this book.

Table of Contents

How Will This Book Help You?

Assuming you are actually on instagram, what have you been using it for? Are you merely following celebrities, friends or other folks, using it just as a hobby or to kill time? While there is nothing wrong with being social and interested to know what people you are fond of are up to or even sharing your life and enjoying yourself at the same time, something is really wrong if you fail to make an extra buck while the opportunity is right in front of your eyes, unless your pockets are too full of course. If you want to make money out of your activities on instagram, this book will show you the tricks, tips and offer you a comprehensive guide to do so. If you are not on Instagram, it will inspire you to join this amazing moneymaking and enjoyable network and possibly make thousands of dollars in the process.

The Basics

"All compromise is based on give and take, but there can be no give and take on fundamentals. Any compromise on mere fundamentals is a surrender. For it is all give and no take."

-Mohandas Gandhi

What is instragram?

According to Wikipedia, Instagram is an online mobile video sharing, social networking, and mobile photo sharing service that allows different users to take videos and photos and then share them on different social networking platforms like Flickr, Tumblr, Twitter, and Facebook. As you can see from the description, it is a mobile app for smartphones and is available on Windows mobile, iOS and Android.

With the app, you can add captions and filters to your photos, get likes, and increase followers tremendously. You can also follow friends or whoever else you like to get their pictures on your Instagram feed.

If you are awfully talented in taking amazing pictures, or want to turn your many followers into customers, there are many ways you can begin to earn money on Instagram.

Brief history of Instagram

Instagram was officially launched around 2010 and three years later became one of the largest and most engaging social networks. It's no wonder why Mark Zuckerberg, the Facebook CEO and founder, bought this photo sharing app for a whopping amount of 1 billion dollars from its rightful founders (Mike Krieger and Kevin Systrom). Most people thought he was crazy. At the time of purchase, Instagram had only 13 employees had less than 22 million active users and no website. It has since grown so fast to currently having more than 300 million active users, definitely more than twitter or Pinterest and over 100 employees. In fact, according to recent research, people are spending more time on Instagram than on Twitter or Facebook. It's the fastest growing social platform in the world and its future is very bright. Just as it has upgraded Facebook's balance sheet, it can upgrade your income. Instagram's social feeds and easy to use editing tools make everyone capable of creating and sharing nice edited pictures today. It has empowered people in unexpected ways, even those who don't bare Bieber, Hilton or Kardashian names. You can use it to share your interests for instance skate boarding, art, and other experiences or just share your photos or videos and make money for such a simple effort. Many big companies are now using this platform to reach out to customers worldwide and their sales have sky rocketed. Companies like Puma are even hiring Instagrammers with massive, profound, and engaging followings at more than $5000 a day to capture photos that display the respective company products.

Key Point

With the over 300 million Instagram users, anything is possible. Think of it as a large billboard in a large intersection where over 300 million people frequent and you will discover that this is an immensely big number of people. So whatever it is that you might want to do whether to gain in popularity or to make money, the potential is limitless!

Basic Tips For Making Money On Instagram

"You can never go wrong by investing in communities and the human beings within them"

- Pam Moore

Like many people out there are doing, you can turn this so called hobby to be a money minting cash cow by following the basic guidelines given below;

Build a follower base

Getting people to follow you is the first step to making money with Instagram. Without the very minimum of a few thousand followers, it will be hard for you to convince any brands to sponsor your posts. Even with the over 300 million users, it doesn't mean that being on Instagram automatically qualifies you to have access to this large number of users; you must strive to get a fraction of this number to follow you. Just like any other product, before you start making sales, you need a market and this is your followers. Here is how:

1) Increase followers; Take all the time you need to expand on the number of your account followers by interacting with your followers and posting unique photos. You will learn more about this in the next chapter of this book.

2) Use hashtags to attract more people. For every photo you take, make sure that it has at least three hashtags that can add to your viewers. The hashtags should speak about the photo, but should be broad enough to show up in numerous searches. Don't worry! You will learn more on hashtags later in this book.

Upload quality images

1) Master your craft; the fact of the matter is that, if your photos aren't so good, people will not be willing to buy them. This may mean many different things to different people, but you need to take quality pictures if you want to end up selling them.

2) Use different cameras; avoid limiting yourself to your phone's camera. With Instagram, you can upload photos taken using other devices; all you need is to transfer them to your phone first. Get yourself a nice camera and notice the significant difference in the quality of photos you take.

Set Up Your Store

Without an online store, you are almost doomed. You can't sell your photos via Instagram directly, so you have to set up an alternative way that people can buy your pictures. Here are some ways you can go about this.

1) Hire a store service; you can sell your photos directly through Services like Twenty20, and so on through their site. You get 20% of the sale and they handle the printing and shipping for you. If you want to avoid dealing with printing and shipping orders, this can be useful.

2) Get your own store; you can use your personal website to set up your own online store. You will definately get more money than you would if you used a hired service, although you will have to take care of orders, as well as shipping and printing the images. For each image you upload to sell on instagram, it should have a caption containing a link to its store page regardless of which method you use to set up your storefront. So that the link doesn't take up the whole caption space, use TinyURL or Bit.ly to shorten the address. Take advantage of apps such as 'HashBag', which automatically identifies and posts any items that have the hashtag '#forsale' on your Instagram account to their respective market.

Market your Products

After you gain followers and therefore in a good position to approach and convince any company, do this:

1) Contact companies; you need to explain and convince your target companies how you can help increase awareness for their brand through your Instagram account. Show them how often you update your Instagram feed and give details on the number of followers you have. Carry some sample shots to display and illustrate you know how to take clear, artistic pictures which can shed some positiveness to their product. Services such as Popular Pays and QuickShouts can connect you with companies, which hire aspiring Instagram marketers.

2) Work out a contract. You need to have a clear written contract indicating matters such as the expected number of pictures you are supposed to take, and bonuses for improved number of followers if

any. To protect yourself from being under-paid by the company you are marketing for, sign a contract.

3) Take quality pictures of the service or product. For sure, you wouldn't like to upload a mediocre or bad photo of a product you are supposed to be marketing. For you to keep the contracts coming in future, you need to play your role as an ambassador for a given product effectively and uphold the expected standards.

You are free to add some personal touches to the photo and in fact, you should. You don't want your followers to feel as if this is just one of those advertisements they would spam so easily if they weren't following you. Your followers need to relate with your image on a personal level.

Turn your many followers into Customers

1) Point followers to your blog or site; you should have a link to your company's or personal website or blog always on your Instagram profile. As you continue to gain more random viewers or followers, traffic to your site will also increase. Emphasize on your skills. You can showcase your abilities and talents on Instagram, including fashion, web development, photography, and several other fields. Update your current projects and latest work on your Instagram feed always. Remember to Use hashtags to attract potential buyers to your image.

2) Take your product's photos. If you run a business that deals with physical items like vehicles, cupcakes or whatever, one of the best ways to advertise your merchandise to new people is through Instagram. Take photos of some of your latest products, then make sure you use hashtags to entice more followers. Some hashtag

examples include product name and use, your company name or slogan. If you have a store page, make sure you link to the product's image comments. Remember to submit the nicest photos you got of the product and avoid those low quality cameras at all cost.

Offer Brand Takeovers

You can earn some good money by doing an "Instagram takeover" as a substitute for sharing sponsored posts on your own account. It's exactly what it sounds like and is all about posting photos on another person's Instagram account. Either you can get temporary access to the person's or company's account or you can be asked to supply photos, additional descriptions and hashtags to them. This works especially well for travel accounts, "We supply 5-7 amazing images to a company or tourism board and they feature our photos showcasing how we see the destination," says Bouskill, an instagrammer.

Sell Your Account

You can sell your account for profit once you have a tremendously successful account. You can even get a six digit for selling accounts that have 500,000 to a million followers.

Key point

Stay active on Instagram to get as many followers as you can, upload quality images of what you are selling, set up an online store, market your great skills to companies, and then turn your devoted followers to customers. Do "brand take over" or sell your account if you please. Don't forget to put the links and the hashtags on your Instagram images or comments. When you do that, you can watch your bank account swell in due time.

How to Build Your Instagram Followers

"The secret to getting results from your social networking is to act like a member, not a marketer"

- Mari Smith

By now you are aware that your followers are everything when it comes to making money on instagram. Keep in mind that you need to be constantly engaged with your audience and show them that you are a real person and not a robbot and that their feedback matters. Here are possible and simple ways you can get new or increase on your current followers.

Follow similar accounts

You have to act as part of the Instagram community and fully participate. This means you need to interact and not just upload photos. Follow the accounts of people who are posting pictures that interest you. You will be able to see their latest photos on your feeds. To avoid overloading your feeds, don't just follow people you see on Instagram blindly. Only follow those accounts that are most interesting.

Comment on and like pictures

You should take some time to like and comment on photos uploaded by the people you are following. Apart from this making the other person feel good, it will also make people see your comment or name and possibly check out your profile. You can get a steady stream of new followers if you stay active consistently.

Reply to comments on your own photos

Don't just read comments then ignore them or forget to answer back. If you want to maintain your follower base, it's very important for you to interact with followers. You must read and respond to any comments you find interesting and even thank your followers if they throw any compliments your way. Take the time to answer properly every intriguing question your follower asks.

Ask your followers questions

Use the photo caption to ask your followers some questions. Your comments section will be more active, therefore draw in new viewers to your photo.

Think about having a call-to-action, such as "Share your story" in the comments" or "Double-tap if you found this funny". This will assist you to increase community interaction with your photos.

Connect your Facebook account

Facebook is currently the owner of Instagram as you read earlier so if you haven't connected your Instagram account to Facebook already, you are definitely losing out on more more potential followers. You will get a double exposure because all of your Instagram posts will be reflected on Facebook as well. Click on Instagram Settings menu to connect your accounts.

Fill out your bio

Don't overlook your Instagram bio like most people often do despite it being a very important part of your Instagram account. By letting people know who you are, it gives them a reason why they should follow you. Include a couple of hashtags related to your bio content and place a call-to-action on your bio as well.

Purchase Followers

1) Find a good seller

Definitely, many websites can offer you followers for some cash. If you have employed all the other tricks in this book but still find yourself desperate for more followers, think about purchasing some which may help kick start your Instagram account. Just ensure that you read reviews of the services before picking the one that suits you best. You don't want a raw deal! Fiverr and other marketplaces have many of these service providers.

2) Select the followers you want to purchase

Most services let you opt from a range of packages, varying from 100 to 1 million followers. Select the package that suits your needs and budget best.

3) Make your account Public

With a private account, you cannot buy followers so make a point of making your account publicly visible. Go to your Profile page tap "Edit your Profile" and change your account visibility settings.

4) Understand the shortcomings

You can get a quick boost from purchasing followers but not without some drawbacks. There is a great likelihood that these acquired strange followers will never interact with your photos or leave comments so your photos can stay a bit bare. You will turn people away if they notice that you have lots of followers but without activity.

Here are few tips on how to use Hashtags

Do your research

Do some research on popular hashtags that fit your niche. Hashtags are short phrases and words that explain and classify your image and they are important marketing tools. An image with a hashtag is easier for people to search and adds your image to current trends. If you want to reach a large number of audiences, you should use hashtags. You can copy and paste the most popular categorized hashtags from websites such as 'TagsForLikes', but don't overdo it. You can use Instagram as a tool to find the most popular trending tags. Most of the time, the most trending tags are "#me", "#love", and "#follow".

Limit the hashtags on each image

Find and add the most relevant hashtags to your image. At most, your image should have 3 hashtags. If you have too many hashtags on one image, your followers may feel like it's somehow spam. So be careful not to overdo this!

Create your own tag

If you have a huge bunch of active followers, you can come up with your own hashtags. This could be your company slogan or name that relates to most of your photos. You will be able to brand your Instagram account, and have a more cohesive community presence.

Geotag your photos

Your fellow Instagram users are attracted to photos from familiar locations. In addition, other photos from that location will emerge automatically as you post geotagged photos. Your pictures will also be seen by other users posting photos from the same location and they may follow them to your account, adding to your exposure and possibly getting you new local followers.

Use "Like for Like" hashtags

You can make use of some of the trendiest like-trading hashtags, such as "#like4likes" or "#like4like", if you want to try to boost your likes; just ensure that if someone likes your picture, you actually like his/her picture as well. This tactic is considered a "dirty" tactic by some people and you may end up losing some followers if you excessively tag this. Yes, this tactic will lead you to new followers, but be aware that they may not be genuine in their interest and could be following you for the selfish motive of getting more likes on their own photos.

Key point

Follow people of interest, comment on and like photos, reply and ask questions, create a portfolio, connect to Facebook and even buy followers if all these fail.

How to Post Memorable Content

"Create your own style...let it be unique for yourself and yet identifiable for others"

-Anna Wintour

You need to create posts that will stick in people's minds for a while. Here are some ways you can do this:

Take unique and interesting photos

This may seem so obvious, but simply taking good pictures is one of the best ways to get followers on Instagram. Instagram is flooded with pictures of people's cats and meals, so have well-shot photos to set yourself apart. Let the pictures you take relate to your audience fully. People are hesitant to follow you if you always post images they can't relate with. It doesn't have to be a "perfect" photo to be good. Good photos are more human and any imperfections make them more so.

Put a boundary on "selfies". You can post some 'selfies' on Instagram but don't let them dominate your account. Your followers don't want to see you but rather want to see your photos. You can seem narcissistic if you post constant selfies and this can put off many followers. Sad as it may be, there is an exception to this if you are very attractive. Posting attractive pictures of your gorgeous self can drive many followers to your account. Still, don't let this take over your content!

Post Every Day

You need to have a new post everyday and post several reasonable times if possible. Your presence must be felt all the time. With this your followers list will grow every day.

Add filters

Instagram became so popular because of the filter options. These filters fine-tune the color of your photos and give them a more "real" feel. There is a variety of filters available on Instagram, so feel free to try out several until you identify the one that works well with your photo. Don't use the same filters too often or your images will start to seem too similar. #nofilter is a popular hashtag on Instagram; if the picture is too striking to even need a filter, use it!

Place captions on every photo

You will be amazed how fast you can turn an okay photo into a remarkable one with a good caption. Your viewers' attention is grabbed by using a caption. The more people you make smile or laugh using a caption, the more you'll retain them as followers. Cute captions or jokes are particularly trendy.

Utilize apps for extended editing control

While you can slightly edit images on Instagram, there are many apps for both Android and iOS that can provide a lot more tools.

Use these apps to darken, brighten, crop, add effects, text, and so much more.

Popular editing apps are Afterlight, Photo Editor by Aviary, Bokehful and Overgram.

Create collages

A fabulous way to show a collection of images or progression is to make a collage to post on Instagram. You can do this using several apps including InstaCollage, PicStitch and InstaPicFrame.

Post your photos at a good time

Since Instagram is an extremely popular service, your followers' feeds are probably constantly updated. Post your photos at the right time for them to be seen by as many people as possible. Make sure you post photos in the morning and after the end of normal work hours. Instagram photos normally stay around a person's feed for 4 hours so if you want your followers to actually see your images, avoid posting them in the middle of the night.

Post Beautiful Photos

Not only do you need to post consistently but you also need to post beautiful images, which are instrumental to increasing your Instagram followers. You can even be featured in media houses for the outstanding photos. You need to inspire people through your photos and not shock them out of your account.

Avoid Posting All Your Photos at Once

The necessity to post photos regularly does not mean you post all the photos you have taken at one go. If you want to post more than one photo a day, make sure they are spread out in the day. Share one photo for every three to four hours. You don't want to make your followers oversaturated with images-keep them yearning for more. Don't just dump all of your photos at the risk of making your followers to start passing over them.

Pick up an Insta-Style

Like most successful Instagrammers, you need to develop a signature style for your photos. Whichever technique or filter you choose, make sure your photos stand out from the crowd.

Extra Tips

In order to have more followers, you need to follow Shoutout accounts on Instagram. If you like one of their photos or follow them, they normally award a shoutout to your account.

Use tagsforlikes hashtags. You can install an app on your Android or iPhone that illustrates a list of hashtags that you can add on your photos in order to get more likes. Make sure you check out the profile of whoever comments on one of your photos or likes your photos, and leave a nice comment or a like on their photos as well. By doing this, you will increase the chances of them following you or leaving more likes on other photos. Just make a point of not posting many photos at a go with random hashtags.

In your Instagram bio, state that you're 'Following Guidelines'. For example, if you mention something like "I am a mega fan of Tailor swift!" chances are you will get many people with similar interests as your followers and then you'll most likely get a whole heap of Tailor Swift lovers following you. The real Tailor Swift might join your list of followers if you are lucky enough.

Follow users most probable to follow you back. For instance, fresh Instagrammers will likely follow you if you happen to follow them. Just make a point of finding out the number of posts in their feeds. If you find one with less than 10 posts, it's likely this person is a newbie who would appreciate an extra follower very much and will probably receive you with open arms.

People will most likely follow you if you have equal (or less) following and followers. With way too many 'following', you might be mistaken for a new Instagrammer and people will less likely follow you.

Don't let people mistake you for a bore; put more tags and posts for your followers more often than just once every 12 hours.

Try to take advantage of peak traffic times on Instagram. Don't wait for people to fall asleep; who will follow you during sleep?

Make a point of asking all your real life friends and family to follow you.

Key point

You need to post interesting unique photos then add filters and captions on them and make a collage of photos. Post everyday at the right time and one at a time, have your own style and limit on selfies. With this, people can't have enough of you!

Basic Photography Tips

"A photograph shouldn't be just a picture, it should be a philosophy"

-Amit Kalantri

After getting a nice camera, don't expect it to work magic for you just like that. You need to make the necessary adjustments to the camera and position yourself correctly for you to produce quality photos. Here are a few basic tips you can begin with:

Keep It Simple but Stylish

Once you are set to take the photo, don't forget that in photography, less is more. Instagram is fast and fleeting just like all kinds of social media. The attention span of your users is short which means your photo has only a few seconds to grab their attention. Don't even try to achieve too much in one photo for you may end up accomplishing none of them.

Concentrate on One Focal Point per Photo

Focus on the specific subject you want your viewer to see; it could be an open notebook, a female model, a coffee mug, a swing set at the park and so on. Viewer's attention among multiple subjects is divided by clutter and it ebbs out their interest on the photo. Move closer to the subject to ensure they cover the whole frame. For a wider shot, you need to position yourself in a way that only the fewest elements possible are present in the photo. Make sure you get rid of any distractions at the background of your photo.

Throw Away Your First Few Ideas

Creativity is a key part of photography. Every shot you take is an idea and it requires a lot of creativity to make it work. Before you find the one that best suits your idea, you have to take like a dozen shots. It's rare that you will hit it in the first time around. That's why for any idea, you need to toss away the first, the second and even the third shot. Ideas that pop in your mind so easily are more often than not the most generic, most clichéd, and most typical. Have you seen any photos on latte art? Of people gazing at their feet while lying on a beach? Of bathroom selfies and boring sunsets? Add a twist when approaching any photo whose subject is commonplace. Try different locations, angles, props, and even colors. There has to be something new and unusual about your photo for it to stand out.

Watch the Lighting

When you are taking your photos, pay attention to the light and note how much light is in your photo and where it's coming from. If you are shooting outside, don't take photos of a subject when the sun is at their back. If you are taking a photo in front of landmark or monument but can't adjust your position further, just use the camera flash to cover the shadows.

Watch Your White Balance

The white balance is set automatically in most digital cameras based on the type of light you are shooting under. If you find your camera has problems detecting the type of light when you are shooting under mixed lighting, you can manually set the white balance to make the photo look more natural. You need to have the appropriate light balance to get good-looking photos.

Learn the Photography Rules

"Anyone can write, but not everyone is a great writer". Never forget that this philosophy applies to all areas including photography. You need to have the most basic skills to take a great photo. Make a point of researching online on more basic guidelines when it comes to photography.

Practice Often

Remember that nobody is born as a top-notch photographer-it takes skills, time and practice. For you to take stunning photos without them looking so amateur like, you need to experiment and practice often. Take many photos and add something new to each of them every time.

Don't Give Up

Don't expect an overnight success with your Instagram photos; over time, you'll get better. More people will begin to notice your photos everyday and one day, you will realize your dreams of taking great unique photos.

Key point

Keep photos simple but trendy with a twist, discard your first few shots, watch the lighting, keep learning, experimenting, and practicing and most importantly, never give up!

How to Apply What You Have Learned

By now you must have learnt something about Instagram and how you can use it to make money and stay ahead of the game. Just as a summary, here is how you can put what you have learnt down to action.

Build a large active following using the tips provided then smartly turn your followers into customers. You need to constantly engage with people in order to close a sale or get a sponsorship deal and this can apply to all businesses. Sell your skills or products to your customers and relevant companies. Whether you are a 'real' photographer, a fashion designer, a writer, or a quality analyst, post your progressive portfolio on Instagram and let the community know what skills and knowledge you have. Also, give your contact details for interested parties to reach you.

Take great unique photos and sell them to related agencies and get a commission for it. Get affiliate links and connect with Facebook. For Amazon, for example, create a link for a product with good shots on Instagram then, you will get a commission every time there is a sale. If you love travelling, you should Instagram good shots of places you visit, and then market yourself as a local ambassador of famous spots or as a tour guide. You can apply this trick to shopping malls, restaurants, and so on.

Remember to use the Instagram and available apps to make your photos great; add filters, captions, and hashtags and edit photos using Instagram or extra tools.

Like in Instagram, make sure everything you do in life is unique in order to set you apart from others-you need to add a little twist and have your own style to always stand out. Learn more and practice often to be good at what you do. Your time and effort will pay out eventually.